AF897654

Photography by John Ruebartsch

For information, please contact:

Innovative Futures Press
544 E. Ogden Avenue, Suite 700-396
Milwaukee, WI 53202-2657
books@davidzach.com

ISBN #978-1-891630-03-3

Although the author and the publisher have made every effort to ensure the accuracy and completeness of information contained in this book, we assume no responsibility for errors, inaccuracy, omissions, or any inconsistency herein.

Quantity discounts are available on bulk purchases of this book. Special books or book excerpts can also be created to fit special needs. Please contact the publisher to discuss additional information and ideas.

dedication

Robert G. Zach, MD
1925 - 1995

Worth Remembering

The future value of old ideas

David Zach, futurist

When I was a boy of about twelve and was digging around in my dad's office, I found a pack of 3x5 cards with quotations on them. When I asked, he told me that I just won't have the time to read everything, so I should look around for the best ideas from the past wherever I can find them and then see what new things could be done with them. He didn't believe in originality as much as finding new ways to combine old things. He said to always look for old ideas worth remembering. A kid of that age doesn't typically remember much of what his old man tells him, but fate conspired for me to remember and believe this.

Since then I've been harvesting these old ideas from hundreds of sources, whenever and wherever I can find them. Most of them relate to the future in one way or another: time, history, innovation, prediction, optimism, hope, curiosity, consequences, learning, family, children, elders and best of all, the sense of wonder that goes with the future. My database of quotes (yeah, I have them in a FileMaker database) is now over 3600 quotations and this sampler is presented as a complement to my talks and as a way to pay compliment to the sources of all these ideas we should remember, consider and share.

I think it's important to acknowledge that quotations are taken out of context. One can hope that your own interpretation is similar to the author's, but words once written are known to wander far from home and find their way into all sorts of trouble. I did try to provide some context by noting birth and death years. Those without dates are most likely our contemporaries whose words are more famous than they.

These quotations are presented as found, so I did not rewrite pronouns to match any modern day sensibility on gender. Nor did I choose them with that in mind. Without question, the selection of quotations presented here is incomplete in many ways. They were collected from the point of view of a small town Catholic boy who loves science fiction and fact, words, books, ideas, exploration, learning and who (never quite) grew up to be a futurist.

I welcome any quotations you might send my way. Please send them to quotes@davidzach.com.

Thanks go to Mike Corriveau, Fr. Jack Gray, Paul Nuccio, John & Jen Zach, Lyle & Julie Maryniak, James T. Harris and Pat Griffin for help with editing, especially to John Angelos, retired English teacher, who still wields a fierce red pen. It is my proud avuncular (isn't that a great word?) duty to thank my niece Jill Zach for the initial book design and Tom Berk for completing the design. More thanks go to the staff at the Alterra, Stone Creek and Anodyne Cafes in Milwaukee for their coffee, bagels and windows to stare out while musing over this project.

The farther back you can look, the farther forward you are likely to see.

Sir Winston Churchill (1874 - 1965)

When thinking about the future, a very good place to start is the past, because it used to be the future and has some experiences to share. If we listen to our ancestors, living and dead, perhaps we can learn and progress can be steady and real. If we try to do it on our own, the future will not be as good (nor as grateful) as it could be.

It is often difficult to remember that events that occurred in the far, far distant past were once in the future.

G. M. Trevelyan (1876 - 1962)

Tradition means giving votes to the most obscure of all classes, our ancestors. It is the democracy of the dead.

G. K. Chesterton (1874 - 1936)

The dead are generally discouraged from voting. This may be wrong, or at least something to philosophically reconsider. We might know their wishes by looking back on their lives. How did they live? What did they favor? What were their mistakes? How much of it was because of the context of their times and how much was despite the temper of the day? We cannot know exactly, but to ignore them and the price they paid to get us to this day would be a sort of temporal arrogance. Those who will someday call us their ancestors will rightly hold us in contempt if we have neglected our own.

History is a vast early-warning system.

Norman Cousins (1915 - 1990)

Those who cannot remember the past are condemned to repeat it.

George Santayana (1863 - 1952)

History lingers.

George Will (1941 -)

Difficulty is the excuse history never accepts.

Samuel Grafton (1907 - 1997)

A good reason to study history is to find precedent and alternatives so we might avoid the constant search for new excuses as well as not repeat old errors. After all, there are so many new errors just waiting for their chance.

There has never been an age that did not applaud the past and lament the present.

Lillian Eichler Watson (1902 -)

It's got to be the biggest ego trip in the world to think we can reject thousands of years of history.

Richard Jenrette (1929 -)

Maybe we're about to radically change the operating system of the human condition. If so, then this would be a really good time to make backups of our civilization.

Bruce Sterling (1954 -)

Isn't this what education is supposed to be? Unfortunately, today's educational content and methods are often younger than the students themselves. With only wandering definitions of progress, the backups are abandoned and the bugs in this sort of software often get redefined as features.

Throughout history the world has been laid waste to ensure the triumph of conceptions that are now as dead as the men that died for them.

Henry de Montherlant (1896 - 1972)

We would like to live as we once lived, but history will not permit it.

John F. Kennedy (1917 - 1963)

Then again, history can also be used to prove just about anything. It proves we can live in a wide variety of conditions and attitudes. Choosing between all of them is the challenge.

Perhaps in time the so-called Dark Ages will be thought of as including our own.

Georg Christoph Lichtenberg (1742 - 1799)

There are certain moments when we might wish the future were built by men of the past.

Jean Rostand (1894 - 1997)

This can be difficult to accept because the present was obviously built by men of the past and a lot of us are rather unimpressed. The questions should be which men, which past and of course, which future?

I'm not convinced that the world is in any worse shape than it ever was. It's just in this age of almost instantaneous communication, we bear the weight of problems our forefathers only read about after they were solved.

William E. Vaughan under the pseudonym Burton Hillis (1915 - 1977)

It is possible to believe that all the past is but the beginning of a beginning, and that all that is and has been is but the twilight of the dawn. It is possible to believe that all the human mind has ever accomplished is but the dream before the awakening.

H. G. Wells (1866 - 1946)

We've really only used up a very small part of the future so far. This game we find ourselves in has only just begun, so don't expect things to be perfect and take a little time to forgive those who aren't perfect — including ourselves.

Forgive yourself every day.

St. Francis of Assisi (1182 - 1226)

And throughout all Eternity I forgive you, you forgive me.

William Blake (1757 - 1827)

In an imperfect world with imperfect people who perhaps are able to hold in their minds the notion of perfection, forgiveness is a virtue that should have fewer limits. Should any of us ever find ourselves in a place of perfection, a history of forgiveness will look really good on the resume.

I like the dreams of the future better than the history of the past.

Patrick Henry (1736 - 1799)

To look backward for a while is to refresh the eye, to restore it, and to render it more fit for its prime function of looking forward.

Margaret Fairless Barber (1869 - 1901)

Here is Edward Bear, coming downstairs now bump, bump, bump on the back of his head, behind Christopher Robin. It is, as far as he knows, the only way of coming downstairs, but sometimes he feels that there is really another way if only he could stop bumping for a moment and think of it.

A. A. Milne (1882 - 1956)

You didn't know that Winnie-the-Pooh was a futurist, did you? Save for the fact that most futurists are not filled with stuffing, we are very much like the bear, and too often we go bump, bump, bumping our way into the future. We really wish there was another way if only ...

Art at its most significant is a distant early warning system that can always be relied on to tell the old culture what is beginning to happen.

Marshall McLuhan (1911 - 1980)

Artists are like futurists because part of artistry is to see things before others can. Too many artists fail as futurists (and as artists) because instead of looking forward, they're looking inward, obsessed with the present and with themselves.

Vision is the art of seeing things invisible.

Jonathan Swift (1667 - 1745)

Poetry remembers the future.

Jean Cocteau (1889 - 1963)

Jesters do oft prove prophets.

WIlliam Shakespeare (1564 - 1616)

Futurists are what court jesters were before that whole royalty thing went out of fashion. We can't really predict the future as much as we point out the obvious in teasing-pleasing ways to busy people who may think themselves the equal of kings if present circumstances were more in their favor.

Acting out the eccentricities of prophets does not make a prophet.

Philip Rieff (1922 - 2006)

Eccentricities can be charming if accompanied by competence, but are pretentious and annoying when they precede it. And, it's just a guess, but I suspect that Dr. Rieff never attended any futurist conventions.

Prophecies of doom are nothing new.

Edward Teller (1908 - 2003)

This is one tradition that modern types can't seem to get enough of. A common eccentricity of intellectuals is pessimism which can only be cured if more people would take them seriously. Please don't do that.

Such things have often happened and still happen, and how can these be signs of the end of the world?

Julian, Emperor of Rome (331-363)

What is prophecy but a denial of possibility, of adventure, of the dream of becoming.

Anatole Broyard (1920 - 1990)

If you are thinking a year ahead, sow a seed. If you are thinking 10 years ahead, plant a tree. If you are thinking one hundred years ahead, educate the people.

Kuan Tzu (7th century BC)

Why is this so difficult to grasp? Is it because we have made the present so comfortable that we don't find enough reason to think across time? Is it just our nature to mostly think in present tense? It is because as children we are often told not to daydream?

Forewarned, forearmed.

Miguel de Cervantes (1547 - 1616)

Wisdom consists of the anticipation of consequences.

Norman Cousins (1915 - 1990)

One clear mark of the moderns is a belief that consequences and responsibility are not easily connected. At first glance this feels like freedom, on second glance it looks like license. Look once more and it really starts to feel like willful self-destruction.

I distrust anyone who foresees consequences and advocates remedies to avert them.

Edward Wood, Lord Halifax (1881 - 1959)

Claiming to be a futurist does not qualify one to make trusted forecasts and remedies. A lot of people who make predictions really just have strong opinions that the future should be what they want it to be. It's egotism extended forward in time. Is there a profit motive behind the prophet motive? If we follow their advice, do they get rich or gain power?

Halifax's quotation is perhaps an paradoxical match for that cautious comment. He served as Foreign Secretary of Great Britain under Neville Chamberlain. His comment here was referring to those who distrusted deals with Hitler and rejected the 'peace in our time' document that Chamberlain held up for the world to see upon returning from a meeting with Hitler and Mussolini. Some predictions really can come true and when ignored, people die.

Only intuition can protect us from the most dangerous individual of all, the articulate incompetent.

Robert Bernstein (1923 -)

It's also intuition that helps us see competence in those not quite on speaking terms with the language.

Beware of false prophets, which come to you in sheep's clothing, but inwardly they are ravening wolves.

Matthew 7:15

Be careful that victories do not carry the seeds of future defeats.

Ralph W. Sockman (1889 - 1970)

This too shall pass.

Dante Alighieri (1265 - 1321)

Prediction is difficult, especially about the future.

Neils Bohr (1885 - 1962)

An era can be said to end when its basic illusions are exhausted.

Arthur Miller (1915 - 2005)

Miller, author of *Death of a Salesman*, wrote most of his work in the second half of the twentieth century and he recognized this exhaustion as he dissected the myths we had lived by. The rational mind-set that would allow us to dissect living things can leave us feeling rather irrational.

If we were logical, the future would be bleak indeed. But we are more than logical. We are human beings, and we have faith, and we have hope, and we can work.

Jacques Cousteau (1910 - 1997)

Futurism seems to pride itself on logic but I have hope and faith that it can overcome this limitation.

This time, like all times, is a very good one if we but know what to do with it.

Ralph Waldo Emerson (1803 - 1882)

While there's life, there's hope.

Terence (d. 159 BC)

We are saved by hope.

Romans 8:24

Hope is one of the great theological virtues that gives support and purpose to our thoughts about the future. It is an easy thing to be hopeful when one can reasonably expect a good outcome. It is when things are reasonably hopeless and we still have hope that the strength of this virtue is revealed.

The test of a first-rate intelligence is the ability to hold two opposed ideas in the mind at the same time, and still retain the ability to function. One should be able to see that things are hopeless and yet be determined to make them otherwise.

F. Scott Fitzgerald (1896 - 1940)

It doesn't hurt to be optimistic. You can always cry later.

Lucimar Santos de Lima (-)

There is hope for the future because God has a sense of humor and we are funny to God.

Bill Cosby (1937 -)

Hope is born of the long night of watching and tears.

E. H. Chapin (1840 - 1880)

Curiosity is little more than another name for hope.

August W. Hare (1792 - 1834)

For him that is joined to all the living, there is hope.

Ecclesiastes 9:4

Optimism is the faith that leads to achievement. Nothing can be done without hope.

Helen Keller (1880 - 1968)

Optimism is an intellectual choice.

Diana Schneider (-)

So how come intellectuals keep choosing pessimism? At least a mix of the two would be preferable and realistic.

No one knows enough to be a pessimist.

Norman Cousins (1915 - 1990)

How many of you know people who are prematurely disappointed in the future? Ask them for their sources. Or even better, try to ignore them.

Pessimism, when you get used to it, is just as agreeable as optimism.

Arnold Bennett (1867 - 1931)

People often ask, "Are you an optimistic futurist?" and I suspect that few would hire me if I wasn't. Sure, I have my fears and doubts, but I believe that optimism is both practical and preferable and the virtue of hope is something of a moral imperative. If people in the past still held hope through all of their trials (they must have, because we are still here) then we must do the same.

Let us not look back in anger or forward in fear, but around in awareness.

James Thurber (1894 - 1961)

The first lesson of philosophy is that we may all be mistaken.

Will Durant (1885 - 1981)

There is one thing which gives radiance to everything. It is the idea of something around the corner.

G. K. Chesterton (1874 - 1936)

The opportunities are still there.

Walt Disney (1901 - 1966)

Fortune favors the bold.

Virgil (70 - 19 BC)

It is absurd to say that the age of miracles is past. It has not yet begun.

Oscar Wilde (1854 - 1900)

The creation of the future is in the hands of those who can clearly identify their own values, conceive goals which embody those values, and devote their best efforts toward achieving those goals.

J. Peter Vajk (1942 -)

In the face of uncertainty, there is nothing wrong with hope.

Bernie Siegel (-)

Beware how you take away hope from any human being.

Oliver Wendell Holmes, Jr. (1841 - 1935)

My interest is in the future because I am going to spend the rest of my life there.

Charles F. Kettering (1876 - 1958)

The ultimate test of man's conscience may be his willingness to sacrifice something today for future generations whose words of thanks will not be heard.

Gaylord Nelson (1916 - 2005)

I believe that man will not merely endure; he will prevail.

William Faulkner (1897 - 1962)

These are the hard times in which a genius would wish to live. Great necessities call forth great leaders.

Abigail Adams (1744 - 1818)

You will always underestimate the future.

Charles F. Kettering (1876 - 1958)

The future lies in the hands of those who are able to give tomorrow's generations valid reasons to live and hope.

Pierre Teilhard de Chardin (1881 - 1955)

It is never safe to look into the future with eyes of fear.

E. H. Harriman (1848 - 1909)

Where there is no vision, the people perish.

Proverbs 29:18

There is nothing more difficult to take in hand, more perilous to conduct or more uncertain in its success than to take the lead in the introduction of a new order of things.

Niccolo Machiavelli (1469 - 1547)

Every beginning is a consequence — everything beginning ends something.

Paul Valery (1871 - 1945)

Stop trying to fix things in the short-run.

Donald Regan (1918 - 2003)

Real generosity toward the future consists in giving all to what is present.

Albert Camus (1913 - 1960)

Americans used to see the future as a sort of earthly promised land wrought through our hard work and commitments. Now we treat it as a sort of raw material we can use to make us faster, richer and stronger today.

We have it in our power to begin the world again.

Thomas Paine (1737 - 1809)

All is flux, nothing stands still.

Heraclitus (c. 535 - 475 BC)

Nothing endures but change.

Heraclitus (c. 535 - 475 BC)

We find ourselves in this modern world of constant change supposing more often than not that change is good. There are also vast populations that seem to believe that nothing should ever be done for the first time. Change is mostly neutral and its implications are little anticipated until quite often it is too late.

Paradoxically, this quotation is only true if nothing is true. If you believe that truth exists, no matter how difficult it is for us mere mortals to recognize it and even more difficult for us to articulate it, then there's reason to believe that not everything changes. If nothing endures, would the words "We hold these truths to be self-evident . . . " have ever been written? And, if those words had not been written, would they still be true?

Begin with the end in mind.

Steven Covey (1932 -)

Progress might have been all right once, but it's gone on too long.

Ogden Nash (1902 - 1971)

All progress is based upon a universal innate desire on the part of every organism to live beyond its income.

Samuel Butler (1835 - 1902)

In the name of progress we have sacrificed an inherent need for quietness, for serenity.

Gianni Bortolotti (-)

The fatal metaphor of progress, which means leaving things behind us, has utterly obscured the real idea of growth, which means leaving things inside us.

G. K. Chesterton (1874 - 1936)

G. K. Chesterton is one of my favorite authors. Writing mostly in the first three decades of the last century, he was a prolific writer and many of his timeless insights seem specifically appropriate for our time. An excellent source for all things Chesterton is www.chesterton.org.

Decadence can find agents only when it wears the mask of progress.

George Bernard Shaw (1856 - 1950)

The art of progress is to preserve order amid change and to preserve change amid order.

Alfred North Whitehead (1861 - 1947)

People are continually told they should be open to change — that they should be "change agents." Well, what if it's a stupid change? Maybe we need "agents of tradition" to counterbalance? Clearly there a lot of those types too, though have you heard of anyone claiming that job description?

It should be clear that not all change is progress. Equally, not all traditions are worth protecting. Progress comes from the ability to choose between change and tradition.

All change is not growth, as all movement is not forward.

Ellen Glasgow (1873 - 1945)

There is more to life than increasing its speed.

Mahatma Gandhi (1869 - 1948)

As the speed of change accelerates, the value of newness diminishes.

Karrie Jacobs (-)

It is a lot easier to be new than it is to be good. The criteria for being new is only based on the past few years, but the criteria for being good is based on everything we have learned since the beginning of time.

Jeffrey Keedy (-)

New stuff is seductive because it often has powerful marketing forces behind it, and too often a sense of boredom with what's already here is driving its next embrace. If a society cannot select, define and defend its best traditions, it's probably not a society all that interested in survival.

There is a certain relief in change, even though it may be for the worse.

Washington Irving (1783 - 1859)

It is of the new things that men tire ... of fashions and proposals and improvements and change. It is the old things that startle and intoxicate. It is the old things that are young.

G. K. Chesterton (1874 - 1936)

There is nothing culturally more subversive than the modern commerce of quick turnover in ideas.

Philip Rieff (1922 - 2006)

No public should be too quickly ready for change. Such readiness indicates a breakdown of culture.

Philip Rieff (1922 - 2006)

There's a modern addiction to change and anything that's new, along with a feeling that anything old or traditional is bad. This is false. Like any other sort of addict, they don't care about the consequences, they just need another fix.

To plan our future in an uncertain world, we must take into account Change and Constancy. The future consists of both elements, despite current emphasis most futurists place on change.

Richard Bolles (1927 -)

I cannot and will not cut my conscience to fit this year's fashions.

Lillian Hellman (1905 - 1984)

In matters of style, swim with the current; in matters of principles, stand like a rock.

Thomas Jefferson (1743 - 1826)

We should play with fads, work with trends, and live by principles. Or at least that's what we should try to do. Unfortunately, too often we find that we are seduced by fads, ignorant of trends, and resistant to principles.

A dead thing can go with the stream, but only a living thing can go against it.

G. K. Chesterton (1874 - 1936)

Unpredictability, too, can be monotonous.

Eric Hoffer (1902 - 1983)

Chaos is dull.

G. K. Chesterton (1874 - 1936)

Change for the sake of change has nothing to do with vision.

Jack H. Summerford (-)

People change and forget to tell each other.

Lillian Hellman (1905 - 1984)

Styles fade, style is eternal.

Yves Saint Laurent (1936 -)

A man of courage flees forward, in the midst of new things.

Jacques Maritain (1882 - 1973)

It seems to me that it should be a well-educated courage that helps decide the direction that one should flee. Towards what? Away from what? The act of choosing clear directions requires courage too.

Men on frontiers whether of time or space, abandon their previous identities. Neighborhood gives identity. Frontiers snatch it away.

Marshall McLuhan (1911 - 1980)

In a time of drastic change it is the learners who inherit the future. The learned usually find themselves equipped to live in a world that no longer exists.

Eric Hoffer (1902 - 1983)

Hoffer is another of my favorite authors. Get this: he was both a longshoreman and a philosopher. Doing day work on the docks, he'd write during lunch and after hours. His classic book is *The True Believer*, and he has ten others that are just as intriguing. He wrote in an aphoristic style, so he's easy to digest and to quote.

Without a knowing why, he lost his sight when he was a boy and only regained it several years later. After that he read everything he could because he didn't know when he might lose it again. Most of his education was outside of school and often guided by the kindness of strangers and a few friends.

The conservative who resists change is as valuable as the radical who proposes it.

Will and Ariel Durant (W: 1885 - 1981, A: 1898 - 1981)

The Durants are also favorite authors. They wrote the 11-volume *The Story of Civilization*, which is pretty much the largest single study of us. They summarized it in a one hundred page book called *The Lessons of History*. In case you don't have a lot of time, this charming book does our history quite nicely.

He was her teacher, she his student. They fell in love, he resigned, they married. She was 15, he was 28. She rollerskated to their wedding. It was a different time. They were married for 68 years, and died within two weeks of each other.

The excellent is new forever.

Ralph Waldo Emerson (1803 - 1882)

To select well among old things is almost equal to inventing new ones.

Nicolas Charles Trublet (1697 - 1770)

Play so that you may be serious.

Anacharsis (c. 600 BC)

With the various scientists, designers and inventors that I've met through my work, I was often pleased to find a defiant playfulness in them. Many would tell me how they had to hide this from their managers.

The creative mind plays with the objects it loves.

Carl Jung (1875 - 1961)

Perhaps imagination is only intelligence having fun.

George Scialabba (-)

Man was shaped less by what he had to do than by what he did in playful moments.

Eric Hoffer (1902 - 1983)

Every time I see an adult on a bicycle, I no longer despair for the future of the human race.

H. G. Wells (1866 - 1946)

It is the child in man that is the source of his uniqueness and creativeness, and the playground is the optimal milieu for the unfolding of his capacities and talents.

Eric Hoffer (1902 - 1983)

When science discovers the center of the universe, a lot of people will be disappointed to find they are not it.

Bernard Baily (1916 - 1996)

It is well to remember that the entire population of the universe, with one trifling exception, is composed of others.

John Andrew Holmes, Jr. (1841 - 1935)

The story so far: In the beginning the Universe was created. This has made a lot of people very angry and has been widely regarded as a bad move.

Douglas Adams (1952 - 2001)

Damn the solar system. Bad light; planets too distant; pestered with comets; feeble contrivance; could have made a better one myself.

Lord Francis Jeffrey (1773 - 1850)

In his day, scientific ability was still a youngster so one can be amused at his arrogance and also have a certain broader gratitude for the confidence in our abilities. The defiance built into human nature has its value, although I suspect his redesign of the solar system might not have been better.

They said it couldn't be done, but sometimes it doesn't work out that way.

Casey Stengel (1890 - 1975)

Torture numbers, and they'll confess to anything.

Gregg Easterbrook (1953 -)

Facts do not cease to exist because they are ignored.

Aldous Huxley (1894 - 1963)

Every man takes the limits of his own field of vision for the limits of the world.

Arthur Schopenhauer (1788 - 1860)

But he hasn't got any clothes on, a little boy said.

Hans Christian Andersen (1805 - 1875)

I believe in the imagination. What I cannot see is infinitely more important than what I can see.

Duane Michals (1932 -)

To see what is in front of one's nose requires a constant struggle.

George Orwell (1903 - 1950)

We do not err because truth is difficult to see. It is visible at a glance. We err because this is more comfortable.

Alexander Solzhenitzyn (1918 -)

With the last few quotes in mind, the essential virtue of hope includes the ability to ignore the facts or at least to limit their power; to see through the obscene and to focus on the invisible. That's a constant struggle as well. It's all about the power of vision, both to see and not to see.

Reality is that which, when you stop believing in it, doesn't go away.

Philip K. Dick (1928 - 1982)

Once a doctrine, however irrational, has gained power in a society, millions of people will believe in it rather than feel ostracized and isolated.

Erich Fromm (1900 - 1980)

I have not failed. I've just found 10,000 ways that won't work.

Thomas A. Edison (1847 - 1931)

I once read that entrepreneurs literally do not get the concept of failure. They understand that one particular thing may not work, but not that it can never be solved. George Bernard Shaw had said that progress depends on the unreasonable. It does not. Progress depends on the entrepreneurs.

What we need are more people who specialize in the impossible.

Theodore Roethke (1908 - 1963)

Our greatest glory is not in never falling, but in rising every time we fall.

Confucius (551 - 479 BC)

There can be no real freedom without the freedom to fail.

Eric Hoffer (1902 - 1983)

The next time someone talks to you about zero defects or total quality, recall this quote. The freedom to fail is one of our greatest freedoms, because it assumes that we are still humans and we can always do better. Only in a dictatorship, where the answers are predetermined, can there be no failure (or they execute and bury them). If you are not free to fail, you are not free to invent, to learn, to imagine or even to play. Failure should be limited, not eliminated.

There's pressure today for humans not to be humans, but to be machines. They are not and must not be.

An essential aspect of creativity is not being afraid to fail.

Edwin Land (1909 - 1991)

It doesn't matter if you try and try and try again, and fail. It does matter if you try and fail, and fail to try again.

Charles F. Kettering (1876 - 1958)

If at first you don't succeed, try, try again. Then give up. There's no use in being a damn fool about it.

W. C. Fields (1880 - 1946)

The only interesting fields of science are the ones where you still don't know what you're talking about.

I. I. Rabi (1898 - 1988)

Basic research is what I am doing when I don't know what I am doing.

Wernher von Braun (1912 - 1977)

The most exciting phrase to hear in science, the one that heralds new discoveries, is not "Eureka!" but "That's funny ..."

Isaac Asimov (1920 - 1992)

The first step is always to succeed in becoming surprised — to notice that there is something funny going on.

David Gelernter (1955 -)

This is a key talent for futurists — to notice what most people miss and to connect the obvious with the unexpected. It's surprising how many people are unwilling to be surprised.

In 1993 Gelernter was surprised by a package sent by the Unibomber. He was critically injured and sustained permanent injury to his right hand and eye. Not too surprisingly, he continues to do math and continues to write.

Discovery consists in seeing what everyone else has seen and thinking what no one else has thought.

Albert Szent-Gyorgi (1893 - 1986)

The "silly question" is the first intimation of some totally new development.

Alfred North Whitehead (1861 - 1947)

We are confronted with insurmountable opportunities.

Pogo (Walt Kelly) (1913 - 1973)

Anything will give up its secrets if you love it enough.

George Washington Carver (1864 - 1943)

I have learned to use the word impossible with the greatest caution.

Wernher von Braun (1912 - 1977)

Whenever you are thinking about some future forecast and believe that it can't happen, step back and ask, "What would have to change so that it could happen?" If you're imaginative, you will find a lot more possibilities.

When a distinguished but elderly scientist states that something is possible, he is almost certainly right. When he states that something is impossible, he is very probably wrong.

Arthur C. Clarke (1917 - 2008)

Dare to be naive.

Buckminster Fuller (1895 - 1983)

Pollution is nothing but resources we're not harvesting.

Buckminster Fuller (1895 - 1983)

However far modern science and technics have fallen short of their inherent possibilities, they have taught mankind at least one lesson: Nothing is impossible.

Lewis Mumford (1895 - 1990)

Whenever you look at a piece of work and you think the fellow was crazy, then you want to pay some attention to that. One of you is likely to be, and you had better find out which it is. It makes an awful lot of difference.

Charles F. Kettering (1876 - 1958)

Of course, you both might be crazy, so you then have to figure out if the craziness is destructive or constructive. That makes an awful lot of difference too. Is it craziness or is it brilliance and insight that's two steps ahead of everyone else? Maybe they're really only one step ahead and you're one step behind.

Give me a firm place to stand and I will move the Earth.

Archimedes (287 - 212 BC)

We haven't got the money. So we've got to think.

Ernest Rutherford (1871 - 1937)

The whole difference between construction and creation is exactly this: that a thing constructed can only be loved after it is constructed; but a thing created is loved before it exists.

G. K. Chesterton (1874 - 1936)

Any sufficiently advanced technology is indistinguishable from magic.

Arthur C. Clarke (1917 - 2008)

If I have seen farther it is by standing upon the shoulders of Giants.

Sir Isaac Newton (1643 - 1727)

One of the best things to come out of the home computer revolution could be the general and widespread understanding of how severely limited logic is.

Frank Herbert (1920 - 1986)

A computer lets you make more mistakes faster than any invention in human history — with the possible exception of handguns and tequila.

Mitch Ratliffe (-)

Computers are useless. They can only give you answers.

Pablo Picasso (1881 - 1973)

We cannot get grace from gadgets.

J. B. Priestley (1894 - 1984)

Technology is sold as a solution but we can never fully forecast the new problems the new solutions will bring. If you bring in a new technology, ask these four questions from the writer Neil Postman:

1. What problem is this technology trying to solve?
2. Is that my problem?
3. By solving this problem, what new problems am I creating?
4. Am I using the technology or is it using me?

Merely having an open mind is nothing; the object of opening the mind, as of opening the mouth, is to shut it again on something solid.

G. K. Chesterton (1874 - 1936)

Have you ever noticed that people tend to be open-minded about things they already agree with? Don't be so open-minded that your brain falls out.

I not only use all the brains that I have, but all that I can borrow.

Woodrow Wilson (1856 - 1924)

Keeping problems to yourself is a quick way to fail. Take your problems outside of yourself and share them with others. It's amazing how narrow our personal perspectives often are and how they can be broadened by adding additional minds to the mix. Don't think outside of the box, think into other boxes.

If you see connections between things, your choices will be less threatening.

Richard Saul Wurman (1936 -)

This should be the essence of futurism, not to predict things, but to connect them. Everything of value is the result of connecting people, things or ideas. Creativity is connecting things which at first glance didn't seem connectable. Which connections are just waiting to be recognized? Which threats fall away when new connections are forged?

The universe is full of magical things patiently waiting for our wits to grow sharper.

Eden Phillpotts (1862 - 1960)

I was gratified to be able to answer promptly. I said, "I don't know."

Mark Twain (1835 - 1910)

To see a World in a Grain of Sand,
And Heaven in a Wild Flower,
Hold Infinity in the palm of your hand,
And Eternity in an hour.

William Blake (1757 - 1827)

I am enough of an artist to draw freely upon my imagination. Imagination is more important than knowledge. Knowledge is limited. Imagination encircles the world.

Albert Einstein (1879 - 1955)

There are two distinct classes of what are called thoughts: those that we produce in ourselves by reflection ... and those that bolt into the mind of their own accord.

Thomas Paine (1737 - 1809)

I do not know what I may appear to the world, but to myself I seem to have been only a boy playing on the seashore, and diverting myself in now and then finding a smoother pebble or a prettier shell than ordinary. Whilst the great ocean of truth lay all undiscovered before me.

Isaac Newton (1643 - 1727)

"What is truth?" said jesting Pilate, and would not stay for an answer.

Francis Bacon (1561 - 1626)

If the stars should appear just one night in a thousand years, how would men believe and adore!

Ralph Waldo Emerson (1803 - 1882)

Ideas shape the course of history.

John Maynard Keynes (1883 - 1946)

In the long run of history, the censor and the inquisitor have always lost. The only sure weapon against bad ideas is better ideas.

Alfred Whitney Griswold (1906 - 1963)

A good idea will keep you awake during the morning, but a great idea will keep you awake during the night.

Marilyn Vos Savant (1946 -)

Nothing is more dangerous than an idea, when it's the only one we have.

Emile Auguste Chartier (1868 - 1951)

The simplest things give me ideas.

Joan Miro (1893 - 1983)

Bring ideas in and entertain them royally, for one of them may be the king.

Mark van Doren (1894 - 1972)

Courage is the power of being mastered by and possessed with an idea.

Phillips Brooks (1835 - 1893)

Nothing is so powerful as an idea whose time has come.

Victor Hugo (1802 - 1885)

How many ideas have there been in the history of man which were unthinkable ten years before they appeared?

Fyodor Dostoyevsky (1821 - 1881)

If you are seeking creative ideas, go out walking. Angels whisper to a man when he goes for a walk.

Raymond Inmon (-)

If your ears are filled with earbuds, I would suspect that the angels can't be heard. Angels are not known for shouting.

One can be instructed in society, one is inspired only in solitude.

Johann Wolfgang von Goethe (1749 - 1832)

A good book is the purest essence of a human soul.

Thomas Carlyle (1795 - 1881)

Literature is my utopia.

Helen Keller (1880 - 1968)

When I get a little money, I buy books; and if any is left, I buy food and clothes.

Desiderius Erasmus (1466 - 1536)

Home is where the books are.

Richard Burton (1925 - 1984)

From your parents you learn love and laughter and how to put one foot before the other. But when books are opened you discover that you have wings.

Helen Hayes (1900 - 1993)

**Without books, God is silent, justice dormant,
natural science at a stand, philosophy lame,
letters dumb, and all things involved in darkness.**

Thomas Bartholin (1616 - 1680)

I do worry that technology will conquer the book. As much as I enjoy new technologies, I find great comfort in a book of paper, ink and glue and have little interest in reading a book if I cannot underline it, write in the margins and make it my own. Like most people who use a lot of technology, I appreciate it, but never completely trust it.

**Without books, history is silent,
literature dumb, science crippled,
thought and speculation at a standstill.**

Barbara W. Tuchman (1912 - 1989)

You think your pain and your heartbreak are unprecedented in the history of the world, but then you read. It was books that taught me that the things that tormented me most were the very things that connected me with all the people who were alive, or who had ever been alive.

James Baldwin (1924 - 1987)

Mao said that power comes out of the barrel of the gun, but he was a thug. Power can also come out of the end of a book — the power to connect, the power to inspire, the power to rise above and to forgive.

It is no accident that books are sacred to civilization. They open the past to us. A book is magical; it transcends time and space.

Daniel J. Boorstin (1914 - 2004)

Books are the carriers of civilization ... They are companions, teachers, magicians, bankers of the treasures of the mind. Books are humanity in print.

Barbara W. Tuchman (1912 - 1989)

One glance at a book and you hear the voice of another person, perhaps someone dead for 1,000 years. To read is to voyage through time.

Carl Sagan (1934 - 1996)

I enjoy reading biographies because I want to know about the people who messed up the world.

Marie Dressler (1868 - 1934)

The man who does not read good books has no advantage over those who can't read them.

Mark Twain (1835 - 1910)

I have always imagined that Paradise will be a kind of library.

Jorge Luis Borges (1899 - 1986)

Many learned persons have read themselves stupid.

Arthur Schopenhauer (1788 - 1860)

As someone who owns thousands of books, I always have this growing knowledge that the more I read, the more obvious it becomes that there is so much more that I do not know — and the sneaking suspicion that others do know! Yet, I am still never so vulnerable as when I am in a bookstore. It's true, this is a gentle madness.

It is not true that we have only one life to live;
if we can read, we can live as many lives and
as many kinds of lives as we wish.

S. I. Hayakawa (1906 - 1992)

Reading makes immigrants of us all — it takes us away from home, but more important, it finds homes for us everywhere.

Hazel Rochman (1938 -)

The library is the temple of learning and learning has liberated more people than all the wars in history.

Carl Rowan (1925 - 2000)

There is no mistaking a real book when one meets it. It is like falling in love.

Christopher Morley (1890 - 1957)

The world, you must remember, is only just becoming literate.

Aldous Huxley (1894 - 1963)

It is a mistake to think that books have come to stay. The human race did without them for thousands of years and may decide to do without them again.

E. M. Forster (1879 - 1970)

There are worse crimes than burning books.
One of them is not reading them.

Joseph Alexandrovitch Brodsky (1940 - 1996)

You may have tangible wealth untold;
Caskets of jewels and coffers of gold.
Richer than I you can never be —
I had a mother who read to me.

Strickland Gillilan (1869 - 1954)

Books are delightful society. If you go into a room filled with books, even without taking them down from their shelves, they seem to speak to you, to welcome you.

William E. Gladstone (1809 - 1898)

I cannot live without books.

Thomas Jefferson (1743 - 1826)

Without education, we are in a horrible and deadly danger of taking educated people seriously.

G. K. Chesterton (1874 - 1936)

Words can sometimes, in moments of grace, attain the quality of deeds.

Elie Wiesel (1928 - 2007)

Do not the most moving moments of our lives find us all without words?

Marcel Marceau (1923 - 2007)

More than kisses, letters mingle souls.

John Donne (1572 - 1631)

To be surprised, to wonder, is to begin to understand.

Jose Ortega y Gasset (1883 - 1955)

Knowledge is power, but only wisdom is liberty.

Will Durant (1885 - 1981)

Knowledge comes, but wisdom lingers.

Alfred Lord Tennyson (1809 - 1882)

And the same age saw Learning fall, and Rome.

Alexander Pope (1688 - 1744)

The surest sign that there's intelligent life elsewhere in the universe is that they've never tried to contact us.

Woody Allen (1935 -)

The primary purpose of a liberal education is to make one's mind a pleasant place in which to spend one's leisure.

Sydney J. Harris (1917 - 1986)

I find that a great part of the information I have was acquired by looking up something and finding something else on the way.

Franklin P. Adams (1881 - 1960)

Only the educated are free.

Epictetus (c.55 - c.135)

I am still learning.

Michelangelo Buonarroti (1475 - 1564)

To be prepared against surprise is to be trained.
To be prepared for surprise is to be educated.

James P. Carse (-)

E pluribus unum.

Virgil (70 - 19 BC)

I may disapprove of what you say, but I will defend to the death your right to say it.

Voltaire (1694 - 1778)

We mutually pledge to each other our lives, our fortunes and our sacred honor ...

Thomas Jefferson (1743 - 1826)

Government of the people, by the people, for the people.

Abraham Lincoln (1809 - 1865)

The world must be made safe for democracy.

Woodrow Wilson (1856 - 1924)

Man's capacity for justice makes democracy possible, but man's inclination to injustice makes democracy necessary.

Reinhold Niebuhr (1892 - 1971)

What has always made the state of hell on earth
has been precisely that man has tried to make it his heaven.

F. Hoelderlin (1770 - 1843)

There's no such thing as a free lunch.

Milton Friedman (1912 - 2006)

We did not choose to be the guardians at the gate.
But there is no one else.

Lyndon Baines Johnson (1908 - 1973)

Who guards the guardians?

Juvenal (late 1st - early 2nd century AD)

It's essential for us to embrace this one. There is so much wealth and power in our modern world and we want to give power to those we believe are good in order to do good, but power does have that nasty tendency to corrupt. Our system of checks and balances must be applied to our efforts to "improve" the future.

With malice toward none; with charity for all.

Abraham Lincoln (1809 - 1865)

The mark of the immature man is that he wants to die nobly for a cause, while the mark of the mature man is that he wants to live humbly for one.

Wilhelm Stekel (1868 - 1940)

If we are to preserve civilization we must first remain civilized.

Louis St. Laurent (1882 - 1973)

I am in Birmingham because injustice is here.

Martin Luther King, Jr. (1929 - 1968)

A great deal of talent is lost to the world for want of a little courage.

Sydney Smith (1771 - 1845)

The ultimate result of shielding men from the effects of folly, is to fill the world with fools.

Herbert Spencer (1820 - 1903)

When liberty becomes license, dictatorship is near.

Will Durant (1885 - 1981)

Men do not differ much about what things they will call evils; they differ enormously about what evils they will call excusable.

G. K. Chesterton (1874 - 1936)

Too much freedom is its own kind of cage.

Patricia MacDonald (-)

Civilization begins with order, grows with liberty, and dies with chaos.

Will Durant (1885 - 1981)

We laugh at honor and are shocked to find traitors in our midst.

C. S. Lewis (1898 - 1963)

History will have to record that the greatest tragedy of this period of social transition was not the strident clamor of the bad people, but the appalling silence of the good people.

Martin Luther King, Jr. (1929 - 1968)

In all the fifty centuries of history the masses had apparently only one chance to show that they could do on their own, without masters to push them around, and it needed the discovery of a new world to give them that chance.

Eric Hoffer (1902 - 1983)

And yet those masters do have their ways to reassert their control with the masses too easily distracted away from things that matter, be that with circuses of the old days or the TV and sports of the modern days. How do we keep a new world from growing old?

When smashing monuments, save the pedestals — they always come in handy.

Stanislaw Lec (1909 - 1966)

The truly civilized man is always skeptical and tolerant ... his culture is based on "I am not too sure."

H. L. Mencken (1880 - 1956)

The industrialized world has a different kind of poverty, a poverty of loneliness, of being unwanted, a poverty of the spirit.

Mother Teresa of Calcutta (1910 - 1997)

The poor man's wisdom is despised and his words are not heard.

Ecclesiastes 9:16

It is easier to resist at the beginning than at the end.

Leonardo da Vinci (1452 - 1519)

This is why the study of consequences shouldn't be left to the futurists. When starting something new try to think about what it will be like when it is old and how quickly will it age? What are the implications of the implications of the implications?

It is such a relief to be told the truth.

Katherine Anne Porter (1890 - 1980)

We are all in the gutter, but some of us are looking at the stars.

Oscar Wilde (1854 - 1900)

To do just the opposite is also a form of imitation.

Georg Christoph Lichtenberg (1742 - 1799)

So many teenagers feel they are being original and independent when they really are part of the mass that simply does what their parents would prefer they not do. Individuality has become the new conformity.

I have come to an unalterable decision — to go and live forever in Polynesia. Then I can end my days in peace and freedom, without thoughts of tomorrow and this eternal struggle against idiots.

Paul Gauguin (1848 - 1903)

You don't have to be a world traveler to know that the idiots can get passports too.

Millions long for immortality who do not know what to do with themselves on a rainy Sunday afternoon.

Susan Ertz (1894 - 1965)

Art, like morality, consists in drawing the line somewhere.

G. K. Chesterton (1874 - 1936)

The basic test of freedom is perhaps less in what we are free to do than in what we are free not to do.

Eric Hoffer (1902 - 1983)

It is a blessed thing that in every age someone has had the individuality enough and courage enough to stand by his own convictions.

Robert G. Ingersoll (1833 - 1899)

You can never get enough of what you really don't need.

Eric Hoffer (1902 - 1983)

How does one embrace this without rejecting much of our modern society which validates you by what you have? Wants are short-term, needs are long-term. When you want something, ask yourself first about its long-term value and implications. You can still get it, but at least you thought about it first. That's a start.

Discipline is remembering what you want.

David Campbell (-)

You have no more right to consume happiness without producing it than to consume wealth without producing it.

George Bernard Shaw (1856 - 1950)

The test of all happiness is gratitude.

G. K. Chesterton (1874 - 1936)

Be glad of life because it gives you the chance to love and to work and to play and to look up at the stars.

Henry van Dyke (1852 - 1933)

The feeling of being hurried is not usually the result of living a full life and having no time. It is, rather, born of a vague fear that we are wasting our life.

Eric Hoffer (1902 - 1983)

No big surprise that most people reading this will agree with it. The frenetic pace set by modern times leaves us with little time to actually question what we're doing. Work is over-rated if it is the only thing that holds your attention and your praise.

It's a mistake to take a time management classes. You can't manage time, it's a dimension and unless you're some really clever physicist, you have no power over it. What you do have some power and control over is your attention. That's what we use to interface with time. Sadly, I've not seen any classes offered for managing attention.

Much unhappiness results from our inability to remember the nice things that happen to us.

W. N. Rieger (-)

Leisure with dignity.

Marcus Tullius Cicero (106 - 43 BC)

The loss of dignity in play is a grave error of modern times. Play has become a subsidiary of work — people who work hard and play hard don't really understand the purpose of play, which is not to be hard. When it hardens, it becomes brittle. It may be true that the outcomes of battles have been won or lost on the playing fields of Eton but it is also true that play, when it is playful, has won many battles on the playing fields of innovation, invention and discovery.

The way to love anything is to realize that it may be lost.

G. K. Chesterton (1874 - 1936)

Simplicity, carried to an extreme, becomes elegance.

Jon Franklin (-)

In walking, just walk. In sitting, just sit. Above all, don't wobble.

Yunmen Wenyan (862 or 864 - 949)

Be not forgetful to entertain strangers; for thereby some have entertained angels unawares.

Hebrews 13:2

Never hesitate to hold out your hand; never hesitate to accept the outstretched hand of another.

Pope John XXIII (1881 - 1963)

All great literature is one of two stories, a man goes on a journey or a stranger comes to town.

Leo Tolstoy (1828 - 1910)

When you find yourself amongst strangers, look around and imagine that there's someone here who, if you could find that person and have a conversation, you would change each other's lives for the better, forever. Talk to strangers. They are not as dangerous as we have been led to believe.

To love what you do and feel that it matters — how could anything be more fun?

Katharine Graham (1917 - 2001)

Whoever blushes seems to be good.

Menander (c. 342-291 BC)

Cease to do evil, learn to do good.

Isaiah 1:16-17

It is a great mistake for men to give up paying compliments, for when they give up saying what is charming, they give up thinking what is charming.

Oscar Wilde (1854 - 1900)

I have fought the good fight, I have finished my course, I have kept the faith.

II Timothy 4:7

If the very old will remember, the very young will listen.

Chief Dan George (1899 - 1981)

Real futurists have children.

Bruce Sterling (1954 -)

Children today are tyrants. They contradict their parents, gobble their food and tyrannize their teachers.

Socrates (c. 470 - 399 BC)

Why should we do anything for posterity; what has posterity ever done for us?

Sir Boyle Roche (1736 - 1807)

Good question. The answer is that posterity gives us some meaning beyond ourselves and our time. We imagine posterity innocent (which it will not be) but I think that our hope is that it may be free from any sins that we in our own time have atoned for and do not pass them on for those who follow. That seems a reasonable thing to do for posterity.

My mother had a great deal of trouble with me, but I think she enjoyed it.

Mark Twain (1835 - 1910)

Be patient with the boys — you are dealing with soul-stuff.

Elbert Hubbard (1856 - 1915)

A child of five would understand this. Send someone to fetch a child of five.

Groucho Marx (1890 - 1977)

The pursuit of truth and beauty is a sphere of activity in which we are permitted to remain children all our lives.

Albert Einstein (1879 - 1955)

Children are remarkable for their intelligence and ardor, for their curiosity, their intolerance of shams, the clarity and ruthlessness of their vision.

Aldous Huxley (1894 - 1963)

Children are innocent and want justice. We are wicked and prefer mercy.

G. K. Chesterton (1874 - 1936)

I actually think that to become really mature is to return to the age of five, to become able to recapture the capacity for absorption, for learning, the tremendous hunger to master skills that you have at five years.

Eric Hoffer (1902 - 1983)

I enjoy my imagination most when I'm able to draw it back towards a time when I knew little, was fascinated by everything and I trusted and loved all the world — except for my brothers, of course.

Adults are obsolete children.

Dr. Seuss [Theodore Geisel] (1904 - 1991)

If a child is to keep alive his inborn sense of wonder, he needs the companionship of at least one adult who can share it, rediscovering with him the joy, excitement, and mystery of the world we live in.

Rachel Carson (1907 - 1964)

The simplest toy, one which even the youngest child can operate, is called a grandparent.

Sam Levenson (1911 - 1980)

My four brothers and I were very lucky to have grandparents who still knew how to play. There was always a sandbox, a garden, unconditional love and homemade cookies. Our grandfather had a workshop where magic was performed with wood and steel, tools and toil. It was a sort of a house of worship because there were always little bits of heaven to be found.

Have nothing in your home that you do not know to be useful or believe to be beautiful.

William Morris (1834 - 1896)

When I was young, I admired clever people. Now that I am old, I admire kind people.

Abraham Joshua Heschel (1907 - 1972)

Every child comes with the message that God is not yet discouraged of humanity.

Rabindranath Tagore (1861 - 1941)

I have met so many moderns who by choice, chance or circumstance have not reproduced. The frequent exclamation of "not wanting to bring a child into this messed up world" seems naive, arrogant and ultimately sterile. To believe that these are the worst of times is to misunderstand these times, to be willfully ignorant of history, and to miss a chance to connect with eternity.

I love little children, and it is not a slight thing when they, who are fresh from God, love us.

Charles Dickens (1812 - 1870)

There is always one moment in childhood when the door opens and lets the future in.

Graham Greene (1904 - 1994)

Grow old along with me! The best is yet to be.

Robert Browning (1812 - 1889)

Old age is the most unexpected of all the things that happen to a man.

Leon Trotsky (1879 - 1940)

Middle age is a bit surprising as well.

Death twitches my ear. "Live," he says, "I am coming."

Virgil (70 - 19 BC)

As we grow old, the beauty steals inward.

Ralph Waldo Emerson (1803 - 1882)

How beautiful the leaves grow old. How full of light and color are their last days.

John Burroughs (1837 - 1921)

One advantage in growing older is that you can stand for more and fall for less.

Monta Crane (-)

Anyone who keeps the ability to see beauty never grows old.

Franz Kafka (1883 - 1924)

We are all mortal until the first kiss and the second glass of wine.

Eduardo Galeano (1940 -)

The future is a convenient place for dreams.

Anatole France (1844 - 1924)

I have had dreams, and I have had nightmares. I overcame the nightmares because of my dreams.

Jonas Salk (1914 - 1995)

There are only two ways to live your life. One is as though nothing is a miracle. The other is as though everything is a miracle.

Albert Einstein (1879 - 1955)

I believe in the ultimate goodness of things.

Robert Louis Stevenson (1850 - 1894)

Experience, which destroys innocence, also leads one back to it.

James Baldwin (1924-1987)

Hope for the best. Expect the worst. Life is a play. We're unrehearsed.

Mel Brooks (1926 -)

When it is dark enough, you can see the stars.

Charles Beard (1874 - 1948)

There are things that are so serious that you can only joke about them.

Werner Heisenberg (1901 - 1976)

Finally, a Heisenberg Principle that even I can understand.

Humanity takes itself too seriously. It is the world's original sin. If the cavemen had known how to laugh, history would have been different.

Oscar Wilde (1854 - 1900)

This doesn't seem true. One thing we do know about the cavemen, uh, cavepersons, it is that they were artists. Because they were good artists, we can also infer that they did know how to laugh because artistry and playfulness seem inseparable. It is we who are uncivilized because we now leave artistry to the professionals and dismiss laughter for the immature and thereby believe that we are serious.

The perception of beauty is a moral test.

Henry David Thoreau (1817 - 1862)

Look at everything as though you were seeing it either for the first or last time. Then your time on earth will be filled with glory.

Betty Smith (1896 - 1972)

One might worry that in times like today when we have seen everything, that we really might be seeing them all for the very last time.

Won't you come into the garden? I would like my roses to see you.

Richard Brinsley Sheridan (1751 - 1816)

The fragrance always stays in the hand that gives the rose.

Hada Bejar (-)

One may live without bread, but not without roses.

Jean Richepin (1849 - 1926)

Some people are always grumbling because roses have thorns. I am thankful that thorns have roses.

Alphonse Karr (1808 - 1890)

God gave us our memories so that we might have roses in December.

James M. Barrie (1860 - 1937)

If seeds in the black earth can turn into such beautiful roses, what might not the heart of man become in its long journey toward the stars?

G. K. Chesterton (1874 - 1936)

Love never fails.

1 Corrinthians 13:8

At the touch of love, everyone becomes a poet.

Plato (c. 427 - c. 347 BC)

Be careful what you love ... What you love, you shall soon grow to resemble.

Bernard of Clairvaux (1090 - 1153)

One of the first things Eros does is to obliterate the distinction between giving and receiving.

C. S. Lewis (1898 - 1963)

Love and time — those are the only two things in all the world and all of life that cannot be bought, but only spent.

Gary Jennings (1928 - 1999)

Where there is great love, there are always miracles.

Willa Cather (1873 - 1947)

"God bless us every one!" said Tiny Tim, the last of all.

Charles Dickens (1812 - 1870)

David Zach is one of the few professionally trained futurists on this planet, having earned a master's degree in Studies of the Future from the University of Houston-Clear Lake. Of course that was back in 1981, which means it's pretty much history.

As a futurist, he's worked with over 1300 associations, corporations and colleges offering insights on the personal and professional impact of strategic trends. In other words, he gives funny, fascinating and thought-provoking talks and workshops about both trends and traditions with technology, business, education, demographics and society.

In his work, he studies history more than forecasts. He doesn't want to tell people *what* to think about the future, his goal is helping them to understand *how* to think about the future. He thinks fascinating forecasts can be fun, but thoughtful, long-term choices between change and tradition are much better.

To learn more about the future or to book Dave for your next meeting,
please visit www.davidzach.com or contact your favorite speakers bureau.

Add your own favorite quotations worth remembering

(and please send them to quotes@davidzach.com)

Made in the USA
Monee, IL
18 October 2026

66035043R00070